Boy Afloat

Kayaking solo around Prince Edward Island

Joseph Simmonds

Copyright©2017 by Joseph Simmonds

Cover Design, Book Design, Photographs and Illustrations©2017 by Joseph Simmonds

All rights reserved. This book or any portion thereof may not be reproduced or used in any manner whatsoever without the express written or spoken permission of the author.

ISBN-13: 9781548738808

ISBN-10: 1548738808

There was a young boater who found,

After constantly flipping around,

That the concept of boating is great when you're floating…

…but not quite so great when you've drowned.

-Prince Edward Island-

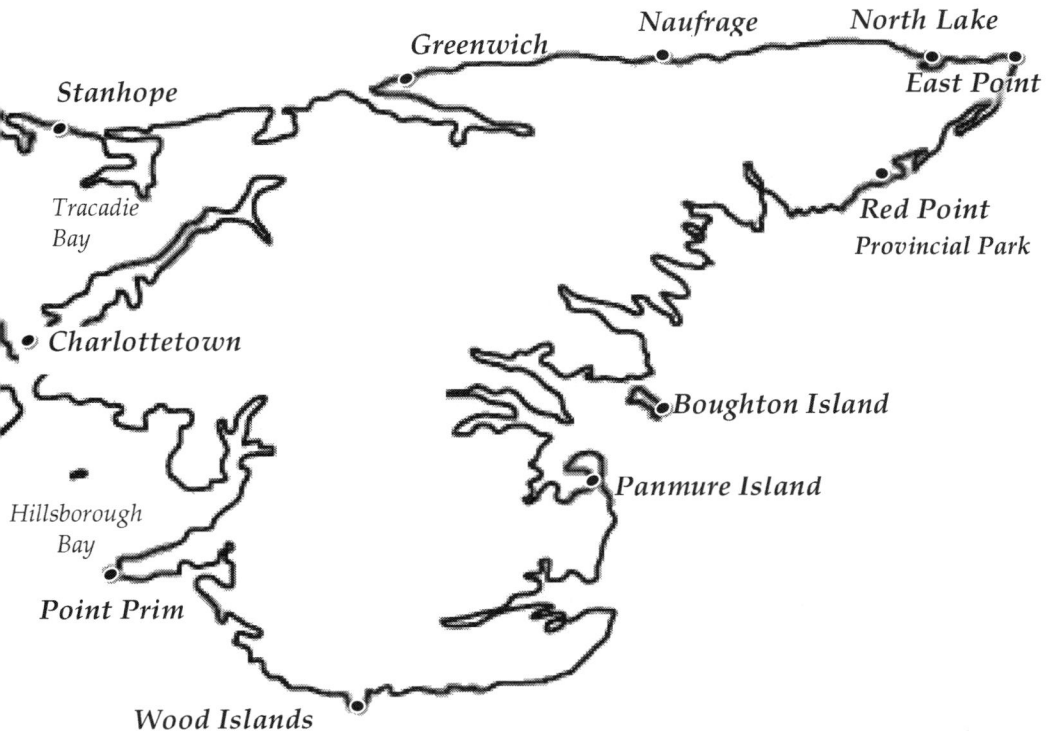

Dedication

To Pat. Without you, this book would not have been written.

To my Brothers and Sisters. Without you, this book would have been finished a lot sooner.

To my Parents. Without you, this book would be a work of fiction.

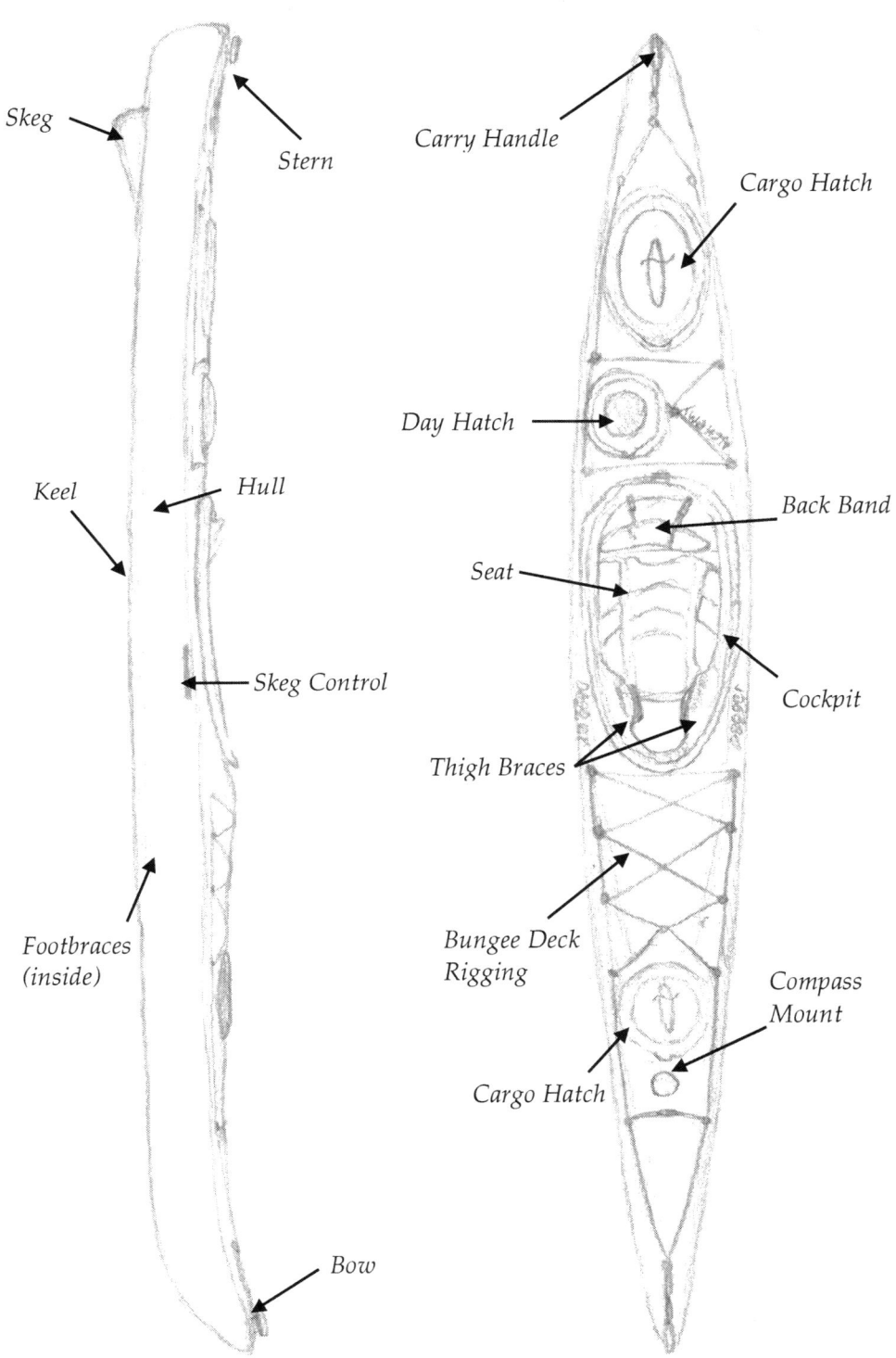

Contents

Introduction…………………………………………………..1

Day One………………………………………………………..7

Day Two……………………………………...……………….13

Day Three………………………………………………...…..17

Day Four……………………………………………………...21

Day Five……………………………………………………...23

Day Six………………………………………………………...27

Day Seven…………………………………………….……....37

Day Eight………………………………………...……..…….43

Day Nine……………………………………………….……...45

Day Ten………………………………………………....……..47

Day Eleven……………………………………………….…...49

Day Twelve………………………………………………..…...51

Epilogue…………………………………………………...…...55

Supplies List…………………………………………………...57

Introduction

Step 1
Inform Dad of intentions.

"Hey, um, Dad?"

"Yep?"

"Can I kayak around PEI?"

"No."

"Come on, I'll be really careful and get all the right gear and-"

"Not a chance."

"Well, I'll let you think it over… you don't need to answer right away."

"That's good to hear."

Step 2
Give Dad some solid facts and stats. Curb his anxiety.

"Hey, um, Dad?"

"Yep?"

"Did you know that the most dangerous part about kayaking isn't even the boating at all? The most dangerous part is driving to your starting point! According to the Canadian Drowning Report, only seven people died while kayaking last year, while there were 1,858 motor vehicle fatalities in Canada alone. Of those few kayaking deaths, not wearing a PFD or lifejacket accounted for approximately 82% of casualties. Of course I shall always be wearing a PFD, so that further cuts down the risk to a barely registering, hardly detectable, frankly miniscule-"

"That's very interesting Jo; maybe next year when you're seventeen."

Step 3
Give Dad some details. Prove that you know your stuff by using fancy kayaker's dialogue.

"Hey Dad!"

"Yep?"

"Alriigght, so here's a map of PEI with my projected daily progress drawn in with red marker. You can see from my plots that the entire trip would only take me around two weeks! Here's a list of the supplies and estimated costs of the food, gear etc. that I would need.

"By the way, I was thinking to get a sea kayak with a skeg rather than a rudder, as I'm only interested in the straight-tracking capability myself. The boat would have a semi-hard chine for ocean stability, be at least 14 feet in length with a nice tight cockpit so that I can perform Eskimo rolls, hard braces etc. without my skirt imploding and would have three waterproof bulkheads as I'd like to have a day-hatch available. I've actually found a beautiful one that matches all these criteria (here's a photo) and what's more, it has the coveted ConTour CFS Seating system!

"Oh yes, for safety I was thinking to bring a phone that has a waterproof ip68 rating with an extremely extended-"

"Look Jo, don't get carried away. I haven't said yes, yet."

Step 4
Just wait. He's obviously coming around.

"Hey, Jo?"

"Yep?"

"You know that kayaking trip you wanted to take? Well, I've been thinking it over… I've decided that maybe I was a bit hasty in deciding that you couldn't go, period. If you show me that you are capable and responsible enough to take a trip of that length, then I will consider it."

"Oh Dad!"

"Just wait. There are some conditions as well. You have to get the proper gear, take a proper sea-kayaking course, learn to Eskimo roll, and take someone with you."

"Oh."

Step 5
Begin to tell people about the trip so that Dad just can't back out. Also, try to convince Dad to ditch the 'proper sea kayaking course' and 'extra person' condition. The course is terribly expensive, and this is something I just want to do by myself.

"Hey, um, Dad?"

"Mhhm?"

"That sea kayaking course you thought would be beneficial for me to take? Well, I was giving it some serious thought and came to the conclusion that-"

"You're going to do it. Without it you're not going."

"Riigght. As for the extra person criteria, well, I know you want- "

"Jo. Look, my conditions aren't changing."

Step 6
Set an official date and begin to collect gear and train like crazy. If you 'forget' about the sea kayaking course, he will too, and if you can't find anyone else to go with you, well, that'll be that.

"Well Dad, I've got everything ready and as you can see from my kayak-around-the-island schedule sheet, my departure date is getting awfully close… Mum even thinks I should leave earlier than anticipated as she's worried that I might have told too many people and attracted unwanted attention. That gives me about three weeks before I should depart. Give or take. It's pretty exciting!

"Oh! By the way, I've been asking around and it's looking like I might have to do this by myself - no one's available. Too bad isn't it?"

"Wait? So you're really doing it? You certainly have a lot of nice gear… Do you want me to look into the best waterproof phone options?"

"That would be great."

Step 7
It's in the bag! Dad's excited now too; I can feel it. The extra person is merely a bad memory, I've managed to transform the proper, two-day sea kayaking course he insisted I take into a two-hour-long rolling session, and as for the emergency GPS satellite tracking and emergency call device he mentioned at one point, well, that's long gone. I'm really going to do it! The only thing to do now is to try to steer Dad clear of any irresponsible-parent horror stories on the news. That could upset the apple cart.

Step 8
Everything's ready. The departure date is set; the gear is collected and packed; I've trained for hours every week, practiced my strokes, braces, rolls and even the art of getting Snickers bars out of the day hatch without capsizing; I've discussed every last detail with Dad and have the necessary safety gear; I've agreed to phone twice a day and give him my coordinates when I camp at night; I've researched, planned and practiced for months on end - and I leave tomorrow.
No chance of Dad backing out now.

Boy Afloat

Boy Afloat

Day One

Monday August 8th 2016
Canoe Cove to Wood Islands (approximately 68 km)
Westerly Wind 25km/h (gusting to 42km/h)

Picture seven people standing on a deserted and very windy beach early in the morning.

The oldest fellow is a tall, thin man with curly black hair and a scattered spray of stubble on his chin. He is the sort of person who always gets selected for those random body-searches they do in airports and ends up getting his belt confiscated and souvenir's destroyed. He keeps glancing around anxiously at the rather fierce-looking waves that keep heaving themselves onto the beach and jangling coins around in his pocket. This is my dad. I think he is having second thoughts about things.

Next to my dad stands my mum. As usual she is principally concerned, not with the fierceness of the waves, the strength of the wind or the fact that I may now be disappearing from her life forever, but with the health and strength of my immune system. On this particular occasion, she tries to convince me to consume a sprig of parsley that she has thoughtfully picked and that she believes will benefit me in some way. I tell her gently that I don't feel like cramming my mouth with a twiggy handful of vegetation right before leaving.

I'm not hungry; in fact, I only eat one bite of a peach she offers me even though it's the nicest, juiciest and most succulent peach I've ever tasted. Little do I know that in a few days I will curse myself for not bringing the peach along and will dwell for hours (for I will have hours to dwell) on the stupidity of my decision.

Nathan eats the peach. Nathan is my younger brother, a pessimist in the truest sense of the word. Throughout my planning and preparing, he has constantly provided me with dark and extraordinarily unhelpful predictions concerning my upcoming fate. If everything goes as he expects it to, my parents will be lucky if the coast guard manages to find my pale, disfigured and sun-bleached remains.

Maya and Toby, the two youngest of the family, stand by solemnly watching the proceedings. Beside them stands Miwa, an exchange student from Japan who is staying with us. I have no idea what she is thinking; for all she knows, this is some bizarre Canadian tradition, a type of Mi'kmaq initiation perhaps; maybe she believes she's witnessing some sort of brutal sea-sacrifice. Whatever her thoughts, she takes lots of pictures.

Abigail, the eldest, is at home engaged in her usual activity of 'being responsible.' Although the chance to see me off is a once-in-a-lifetime opportunity, she doesn't want to miss her ride into work which is, incidentally, picking and cleaning vegetables at an organic farm. I believe I once saw Abigail reviewing study flashcards as she swept the hall, listened to classical music and brushed her teeth, but I can't be sure.

I finish putting the last couple of items into my boat and then hug everybody as quickly as their love will allow; I am dying to start. This is something I have been wanting to do for several years and finally, finally the hour is here. I drag and then float my gear-stuffed boat into the breakers. Waves begin to wash over the bow as I get in. I push against the pebbly sand and with a grating groan the boat is floating, and I am off.

Everybody runs down the beach and then up onto the red-rock cliffs. They wave, not until I am out of sight, for that would probably take them an hour or so and would be a total waste of time and strength, but for a good few minutes anyway. It is nice to have such a fine departure-party, but it is not until they have all slowly walked away that I feel totally free and happy. At last, just me, my boat and the sea.

It is a very windy day with gusts above 40km/h and huge, muscular waves. The wind is in my favor, pushing me from behind, and although this definitely helps me in terms of speed, it does nothing to increase my stability and everything to increase my blood pressure. When you are going against the wind, crashing into waves, not only does the boat remain more stable, but you also feel like you're going faster. When the waves are attacking you from behind, you feel sluggish as all the waves pass you and the boat becomes unstable and hard to control. The whole setup gives you the unpleasant sensation that you are kayaking in a sea of jelly. The first few hours of paddling are tense, panic-filled hours. Wave after wave threatens to capsize me and smash me casually against the red-rock cliffs. There are many close calls, and I find myself constantly saying things like *'That's it, that's done it, it's over!'* or *'Ohh! No, no, not here!'* through clenched teeth.

When I finally reach St. Peter's Island, subdued and rather shaky, the thought of the upcoming thirteen-kilometer paddle across the open water of Hillsborough Bay no longer appeals to me. The waves look hostile, the wind is strong and the distance is…distant. I almost decide to take the safer, longer route around the edge of the bay, but the thought of the extra time that would take dissuades me and I head out.

When I was asked prior to leaving what I would do if I tipped out at sea, I answered nonchalantly, "Oh, climb back in; it's not difficult." After an hour or two of constant paddling, several kilometers from land of any kind, I see that it would not be that easy. Sure, I had practiced re-entering my boat many times in *calm* water and had found it easy enough, but getting back into a sea-water-filled, polyethylene banana while being thrown up and down like a bouy? It would probably be as much as I could do to keep my head above the waves, let alone perform any fancy maneuvers. Having to phone for help on the first day of my trip would be the ultimate embarrassment, something Nathan would never let me forget, so I just grit my teeth and promise myself that I won't flip.

Every time an especially big wave hits me, this is what happens: First, the nose of the boat drops down and disappears into the sea, giving me the first intimation of the horror to come. Then the back of the boat is lifted up into the air, so that I have to lean back, paddling and bracing madly as the huge wave gradually engulfs the entire kayak, frothing around my waist so that only my torso and terrified face are left above the waves. Then, when the wave has finally had enough of me, it suddenly rockets forward, leaving me in its turbulent wake trying to get my shuddering, spinning boat perpendicular to the waves before the next giant swell hits.

This constant barrage of unexpected monster-waves leaves me in a perpetual state of fear and apprehension, and by the time I near the far shore, my hands are shaking, my eyes are wide and every single one of my hairs is standing up on end - although that probably has more to do with the strong wind that was blowing through it.

When I do reach the far side of the bay, I am at a spot quite a distance from the point. I am forced to paddle a good kilometer into the wind before I can relax, therefore, and every time I pause for a breath, my boat slides slowly backward. As I fight against this, I try to remove my sun-hat, but as I do, the strap catches my sunglasses, they flip into the air, and with a sickening 'plop' they disappear beneath the waves. When I think of it now, it still makes me cringe and massage my temples – both the carelessness of it and the memory of the terrible headaches that were to arise because of that senseless move.

Finally, I reach the strip of beach next to Point Prim lighthouse and climb up to the picnic tables overlooking the sea to eat my lunch. I bring the remains of my island map with me and scrape the inky, pulpy mass from my waterproof map-case into a garbage can. I grab a handful of new maps from the lighthouse information desk.

The sea after Point Prim is very calm compared to the wild crossing of Hillsborough Bay, but the sun has decided to take advantage of my un-sunglassed eyeballs. Slowly, my early morning catches up with me, and I feel sleepier than I ever have. I paddle slowly and methodically onward, but every once in a while, I lay my head on the spray deck as I continue to paddle. I actually fall asleep a couple of times, but the sweet respite only lasts a second or two before a wave jerks me back into consciousness. I begin to feel very miserable and the knowledge that this is just the first day of what will probably be a two-week trip almost drives me to despair. While I am fighting with this sleepiness, I suddenly remember that I have a tube of lifesavers in my hatch (courtesy of Mr. Peter Hicks). I quickly fish them out and proceed to suck them one by one as I paddle. I think I can safely say that those lifesavers saved my life, for after eating the entire packet in under ten minutes, I perked right up and was soon paddling happily along.

    Having something interesting to look at makes a big difference when you're kayaking; if you just have the methodically rolling waves to stare at as you paddle on for hours on end, you quickly become depressed and irritable, and your brain begins to sort of decompose, but if you have beautiful coastline, boats, birds or buoys to stare at, then the hours pass by much more quickly. As I near Wood Islands, I begin to see all kinds of interesting things. There's nothing like watching seabirds diving into the water and sending up plumes of spray to lift your spirits.

    I dither a bit before shooting across the entrance to the Wood Island's ferry harbor as I don't want to get caught in the way of the boat and have to pay an enormous fine or something. As it happens, I only just reach the safety of the shallower waters before the ferry gives its terrific screech and comes roaring out. It moves a lot faster than I would have expected, and it is soon entirely out of sight. It's getting late, so I move in a little closer to the shore and scan the coast for a suitable camping spot. There are a lot of cottages spattered along that part of the coast, but I eventually spot a lovely little white-sand beach that lies between two cottages that look empty, so I run my boat onto the sand to investigate.

    An hour later, my tent is up, my macaroni and cheese has been cooked and consumed, my kayak is safely nestled amongst the dune-grass and Dad has been successfully phoned and coordinated. I have made more progress than I had expected and am feeling encouraged. I get into my sleeping bag, zip the door of my tent closed, kill a mosquito and shut the flashlight off.

In the darkness, I eat a Snickers bar.

Day Two

Tuesday August 9th 2016
Wood Islands to Bougton Island (approximately 45 km)
North West Wind 15-20 km/h

I wake up to perfect kayaking weather.

Before setting off, I mix up a bottle of my powdered protein shake that I am supposed to drink for breakfast. It tastes absolutely terrible, warm and lumpy, with a badly simulated chocolate flavor that almost makes it worse. I manage to choke down a few foul mouthfuls and then shove the bottle under the bungee in a likely-to-fall-off-accidentally sort of way.

Since my sunglasses are somewhere at the bottom of Hillsborough Bay, the first few hours of paddling are painful and I am forced to keep my eyes fixed on the deck with only occasional upward squints to make sure that I'm heading parallel to the coast. For some reason, it never occurs to me to put sunscreen on. It doesn't for some time...

As the sun gets higher and I am able to look ahead without searing my eyeballs, I begin to play a game I call 'Paddle to the Point,' which involves guessing how many strokes it will take me to reach a certain headland and then allowing myself to have a Snickers bar if I'm correct. It always takes far more strokes than I estimate, but I eat several Snickers anyway.

I near Panmure Island, a beach I have decided to stop at, and begin to really power-stroke toward it. There are hundreds of people on the beach, and right before I land, I take a quick photo of myself and then check it to make sure I look presentable. I don't, but nothing I do to my stiff, salty hair is of any use, so I give up and land in a secluded spot.

As I pull the kayak onto the beach, a dog-walking lady asks me where I have come from. I suppose it's obvious that I've come from a fair distance; my clothes are disheveled, my hair is a mess, and my boat is engulfed in a tangled assortment gear. I tell her that I have come from Canoe Cove, that I plan to kayak around the Island and that this is my second day of paddling. She looks duly impressed and walks on.

As I begin to pull things out of my hatches, a man comes over and asks me more or less the same thing. I explain once more. He seems very interested, and we continue to talk as I try to locate items from the dark, damp depths of my hatches. Finally, I have everything I need and head off to the bathrooms in order to have a shower, charge my phone and refresh myself generally. On the way, I have to pass through masses of people, and they all look at me rather strangely. It's amazing how weather-beaten you can get after only two days of paddling.

After my shower, I decide to head over to Boughton Island before dark and camp there; the idea of camping on a deserted island sounds thrilling, and so, checking and then double-checking my map to make sure that I have enough time before dark, I head over.

Boughton Island is a lovely little place. Half of it is a high, sandstone cliff covered with stunted, gnarly trees which are in turn covered with nervously shifting herons; the other half is low-lying, with a beautiful white-sand beach. The beach is unfortunately littered with, well, litter, and the sand is covered with thousands of footprints, so perhaps it's not always so deserted after all. As a side note, the day after my stay on the island, the Nature Conservancy kayaked over and cleaned up the whole thing, collecting over 800 buoys.

I phone Dad to let him know where I am and he gives me some information about the history of the place; apparently, it used to be home to a lobster cannery but has been deserted since WW II. After I set up my camp, he calls me again to let me know that if I decide to have a wander, I had better watch out for old grass-covered wells as there are some of them on the island. I assure him that I will be careful.

I pitch my tent directly on the sand which I'd been warned not to do because of rats (courtesy of Mr. Peter Hicks), and although I do hear some strange rustling, scuffling noises during the night, my flashlight doesn't reveal anything, and all in all I have a comfortable sleep.

Boy Afloat

Day Three

Wednesday August 10th 2016
Boughton Island to North Lake (approximately 58 km)
South West Wind 15-25 km/h

Upon waking, I vow never, ever to pitch my tent on the sand again. Having to cram fistfuls of wet, sandy tent into a tiny bag the size of a toddler's sock, and then follow that up with a jumbled assortment of gritty poles and stakes is an ordeal that no one should have to endure.

I decide to cut straight across to Red Point Provincial Park, which is a crossing of almost thirty kilometers.

Nothing particularly interesting happens. I just paddle. On. And on. The water is perfectly smooth, the air is perfectly still, the sun is at a just-hot-enough-to-melt-lard sort of temperature, and there are no birds or seals or boats to occupy the attention.

When I reach the middle section and am several kilometers from land of any kind, it doesn't feel like I'm moving at all. Every once in a while, as a particularly acute feeling of desperation washes over me, I suddenly sit up straight and paddle furiously with gritted teeth and little grunts of determination, but mostly I just sit slumped in a state of congealed jellification, my depression only broken from time to time by the consumption of a Snickers bar.

But oh! The bliss of finally reaching a long-desired point! The feeling of sheer jubilation you experience when your destination is finally tangible and not just a smudge on a soggy map! As I ride the breakers onto the lovely sheltered beach of Red Point, I feel like shouting, running around and clapping random people on the back, but the glum, suspicious looks I receive from the few beachgoers restrains me, and I have to resort to grinning maniacally.

I pop into the campsite at Red Point to charge my phone and have a shower, as by now my arms are encrusted with a chalky layer of salt. I also grab another handful of PEI maps (thank goodness, they're available practically everywhere) and wander around enjoying the atmosphere of populated campground.

The next section of kayaking is wonderful, probably the best conditions I've ever encountered. The coast is fairly straight, so I can stick close to the beautiful, rolling, white-sand beach, and the sea is crystal clear, with lovely foaming waves that are just big enough for fooling around in. I pass Basin Head with its tourist-choked waters, and the huge-home district with its rows of gigantic, beach-side mansions. Suddenly, I notice that my phone has no signal. I begin to get a bit worried. It is becoming rather late, and if there is no signal here, then there certainly won't be any farther east where I am headed. Hoping that I can get through at the lighthouse on the tip, I hurry on. The white sand slowly changes to red cliff, and the huge houses to tiny shacks.

Finally, I reach the East Point Lighthouse and manage to scramble up the cliff. There is still no signal. Just then, I see someone I know - a lady named Carla, coming out of the gift shop. It is quite a relief to see a familiar face at a time like this. I greet her and quickly explain my dilemma. She is surprised and impressed that I am kayaking around PEI, and although neither her nor her husband's phones work either, they promise to give my parents a ring as soon as they get a signal. Richard (her husband) also gives me 20 dollars and tells me to get myself something to eat. Feeling much improved, I head over to North Lake and reach it in good time.

I still want to call Dad though, just to put his mind at ease, but there is no service at North Lake. I ask some friendly fishermen whether they know where I can get a call through, and one of them lends me his phone. The phone smells so strongly of fish that my brief exchange with Dad is rather nauseating, but I am glad to get through. Finally, I can relax.

After setting up my tent on the small strip of beach next to the harbor entrance (contrary to my earnest desires, the sand is the only option), I go for a wander. It is lovely to walk around the boatyard and see the sights, and smell the smells. All the fishermen are finishing up their day's work, washing down boats with pressure hoses or dumping ice from buckets onto the cement. Seagulls are everywhere. North Lake's main industry is tuna fishing; in fact, it's known as the tuna-fishing capital of the world, and fish weighing over 1000 pounds are regularly caught here.

There is a tiny motel with an even tinier café next to it (*The Pirates Boathouse*), and I order a sub and a root beer from the friendly lady behind the counter. As I leave the restaurant, she asks me where I'm from; as quietly as possible I tell her that I'm kayaking around PEI, but she gasps loudly and then proceeds to tell everyone else in the restaurant about my exploit, inserting the words "brave," "amazing" and "young" with embarrassing rapidity throughout the explanation. Trying my best to be polite, I slink out as quickly as possible.

Boy Afloat

Day Four

Thursday August 11ᵗʰ 2016
North Lake to Greenwich (approximately 48 km)

I wake up to the sound of fishing boats motoring out of the North Lake Harbor and the overpowering smell of cold beef sub. I was somehow only able to eat half of the huge and delicious sandwich the night before, and so the other half has been lying in my tent's ceiling-rack all night, infusing my bedroom with a beefy, mayonnaise-y smell. This has given my brain the unpleasant misconception that I have been gorging on sandwiches all through the night and so, without any regrets, I leave the sub on the wooden pilings for the seagulls; it will make a nice change from tuna. As there is no phone service, I set out briskly.

Although I keep checking the phone throughout the day, I get all the way to Naufrage with no service. As I assume my parents are probably getting worried, I pop into a restaurant called *The Shipwreck Point* and use their phone to let Mum know that I haven't drowned yet. I found out later that Nathan, seeing the words "shipwreck" emblazoned on the phone's caller ID screen immediately feared that some catastrophe had befallen me, and that he was being contacted by some sort of emergency response team. He was probably pretty disappointed when he heard the truth. On my way back down to the beach, I buy a chocolate milk and finish it before I reach my boat. For some reason, I've been craving a chocolate milk, probably because the 'chocolate-flavored' protein drink I'm supposed to have is so foul.

Although the coastline is rather dreary (just one long line of crumbly red cliff), there are many huge, imposing houses built along this particular section of coastline, and looking at them and wondering how long they have before the rapidly eroding cliff deposits them into the sea helps to pass the time. Did the builders realize that, on average, one foot of our Island's coastline disappears every year? I pass the most expensive house on PEI that was at one point on sale for 8 million.

Finally, finally, my phone gets service once more and I am able to relax again. I call Dad to let him know where I am, and he suggests that I should try to get to Greenwich Provincial Park before dark. You're not actually supposed to camp on a National Park beach, so I try to beach my boat just outside the official park border. I stick my paddle into the sand to mark my territory and then walk over to see if the showers are still open. The caretaker is just locking them up. When he realizes that I don't intend to leave, he asks me whether I'm camping. He's a nice fellow and is very excited when I tell him about my trip. He comes over and has a look at my kayak and gear and asks questions that I am pleased and proud to answer; he's a kayaker himself, and says that he has always wanted to do the round-the-island-thing. He wishes me luck.

I eat a saucepan full of instant mashed potatoes before bed. The packet says 'serves four,' but it must be a misprint.

Day Five

Friday August 12th 2016
Greenwich to Stanhope
(approximately 49 km - only 33km of actual progress)
Northerly Wind 20km/h (gusting to 37km/h)

The wind is against me all day. I manage to make fairly good time despite it, however, until about 12:30, when in a matter of seconds the wind shifts from being a bracing breeze to being an incredibly strong gale. It's quite fun for a while actually; the rain and spray and howling of wind in the ears makes it thrilling, and I'm not in any danger as I have stuck close to the shore. Soon though, the excitement wears off and I begin to tire. I'm only wearing a t-shirt and so I'm frigid, and what's more, I don't actually appear to be moving anywhere except, well, maybe backwards.

Although I don't want to land and put a jacket on, as that would mean I would never get back out through the wind-whipped surf again without tipping, I eventually have no other choice, and so land in the middle of an island that sits in Tracadie Harbor. I quickly put some more warm clothing on, eat a packet of crackers and so soon feel much better, but I then have absolutely nothing else to do. I'm on an island. I can't go back out until the wind calms down as I would certainly tip, and I can't just sit here doing nothing. I eat a couple of Snickers bars and write *HELP!* in the sand with the end of my water shoe.

Finally, I decide to pull the kayak across the island and enter the water on the other side, in the bay, where it's calmer. I know that there's a campsite somewhere on the edge of Tracadie Bay where some friends of mine (the MacLeans) are staying, and so I decide that I might as well say hello to them while I wait for the bad weather to pass. It takes a long time to pull the heavily laden kayak across the island, and I have to take frequent breaks, but I finally make it.

The water behind the island is vastly different from the mad smash of water I have just left. It is covered with a fuzzy layer of mist, and long lines of multi-colored buoys bob gently in the barely rippling water. I speed silently down the long aisles these buoys create, trying to maneuver in and around this multi-colored maze without smacking into the walls. When I do, I send up clouds of peeping little birds.

When I reach the campsite, I find the MacLeans' camper, but no MacLeans. In fact, there's hardly anyone anywhere - just long lines of campers and RV's sitting sadly and damply in the mist. I take advantage of the emptiness to recharge my phone and take a long, hot shower in the empty shower-rooms. Not sure what to do next, and somewhat discouraged after my fruitless meander, I try to call my parents. My phone however, suddenly decides not to have any service.

How I hate unresponsive technology! Technology is supposed to make things easier, safer, and more hassle-free, but so far, the hardest and most taxing part of my trip is proving to be the constant worry that I will not have phone service, and so will be looked for by the coast guard and humiliated. I wish I was able to just ditch my phone and be completely free from the constant pain that is modern communication.

Anyway, since I think I should probably call, I try to use the camp's pay-phone, but it is even more discouraging. It just sits there looking smug, arrogantly spitting perfectly valid quarters out one after the other until I feel like grabbing it and ripping it from its little box. Just when I've had enough and start to walk away however, it quickly offers me some encouragement in the form of a faint beep or the indecipherable muttering of an annoying lady's voice…your call cannot be…forwarding center…please hang up and try…area code…etc. and I am forced to try again. I leave the campsite in disgust and head back to the sea, which I am hoping has calmed down.

The tide has gone out, and I keep getting stuck on sand bars in the bay. I have to pull the kayak for large distances, a job I really feel I have had enough of for one day. Just before I reach the ocean, the phone regains its phoning capabilities and I give Dad a quick call. We decide that I should camp at the Stanhope campsite if I can reach it before dark. A real campsite! I agree that it would boost my morale, and begin paddling madly along the coast. In my desire to reach the campsite before dark, however, I strain too hard and snap one of my foot-braces. A foot-brace is very important in a kayak as you have to push against it whenever you take a stroke, and not having one makes paddling a lot harder. Thankfully, there is a tiny, spiky stump left and my irritated leg is just able to get enough leverage against that.

By now the sea has grown somewhat calm, and so, just before sunset, I reach the campsite without mishap. The young fellow at the desk looks at me rather strangely. I found out later that they aren't really supposed to sell camping spots to people under 18, but he sells me a plot and doesn't ask any questions.

Campsites have wonderful atmospheres; it's really nice to be amongst happy people, smoky fires, and delicious smells, even if none of the people know or care about you. I am soon able to forget that I have hardly made any progress today and am able to dry all my wet clothes, have a hot shower, charge my untrustworthy phone, have another hot shower, cook a spicy pepperoni rice dish into which I accidentally cut up the plastic wrapping on the pepperoni, and set up my tent on the strip of hard-packed gravel that has been provided for me.

Boy Afloat

Day Six

*Saturday August 13*ᵗʰ *2016*
Stanhope to New London Bay (approximately 35 km)

I wake up early in order to have a third hot shower. The entire campsite appears to be asleep, so I try to take my tent down as quietly as possible. Repacking my boat more neatly and scrunching up a tarp to use as a make-shift foot-brace, I set off. My plan is to meet up with my family at Cavendish beach in order to re-supply, so with great excitement, I paddle like crazy for Cavendish.

The island map is surprisingly accurate as far as the coastline is concerned, but it's very difficult to pinpoint *exactly* where you are; what looks like a flat stretch of coastline on the map can look like a cove-and-headland-riddled stretch when you're actually there. After what feels like an age of thinking it must be just around the next bend, I spot a section of coast that is crawling with garish color. I speed towards it and land on a beach that is plastered, piled and packed with an incredibly diverse assortment of wet and sandy individuals. I pull the boat across the sand, around the sunbathers and through the dilapidated remnants of shell and seaweed-covered sand-castles.

As I walk up the boardwalk towards the car-park, I manage to spot my family. Dad and Abigail are lugging a huge, red cooler between them; Mum is trying to smear sunscreen onto Maya's scowling face; Miwa is rapidly using up what's left of her camera memory; Nathan is attempting to run along the boardwalk railing and Toby is trying to imitate him and almost killing himself in the process. The first things I remember everyone saying are recorded below:

Dad – It's so good to see you!
Mum – You haven't been wearing sunscreen!? Jo-o, really, I thought we talked about this...
Abigail – You look like one of those guys who gets shipwrecked and has to live on a desert island for several years.

Miwa –Say chleese…
Nathan –Your whole face is peeling off! Maybe you'll get some sort of disease.
Maya – Mr. Hicks wanted to come too, but he was busy.
Toby – I cleaned our bedroom.

It feels wonderful to be able to relax for once, eat real food and refresh my weary spirit with a time of real conversation and not just the deranged and muttered monologues of a tortured mind. Unfortunately, my entire face looks like the top of a crème brulee and I am reminded over and over again to wear sunscreen. The reminder is unnecessary, for I had remembered all right after the first couple of days.

After our picnic lunch, I make several trips from van to boat, re-stocking with Snickers, granola bars, Gatorade and macaroni and cheese. Rather than grabbing more cans of Protein shake powder though, I leave most of mine behind, as I haven't been drinking very much of that. Mum and I then give the kayak a thorough overhaul, shaking everything out, drying clothing and collecting fistfuls of licked-clean Snickers bar wrappers. I try to pack everything back into the boat as slowly as possible. I really don't want to keep going. It's not the constant paddling I dread and certainly not the possibility of danger, it's just the being all alone for another whole week. Seeing my family has reminded me how much of a social person I am.

Mummy blows the sand out of my Waterproof Bible and Dad reads a psalm and then we pray. I feel thoroughly wretched and miserable. I slip on my new pair of sunglasses to hide my teary eyes. After hugging everybody, I drag my boat into the breakers, jump in, stretch my spray skirt around the cockpit and push off.

As soon as I get a good distance away from the shore, my dismalness evaporates, and my excitement returns. Unfortunately, my skeg is not deploying due to sand jammed inside the housing, but I have to press on nonetheless. This, coupled with my broken brace, makes it very difficult to paddle straight.

The coastline is superb around Cavendish. I pass New London Bay, one of my favorite spots for sea-kayaking and encircled by one of my family's favorite beaches. I pass the New London Bay and Cape Tryon lighthouses, and try to avoid getting smashed against the huge, imposing cliffs they stand on. The cliffs are crammed with thousands of screaming sea-birds and streaked with white droppings. The birds wheel around overhead and dive into the sea in what appears to be sheer jubilation.

The cliffs seem to stretch off into the distance for a long way without breaches or beaches, and I rush on, hoping for a break in the impenetrable wall. Suddenly I see a tiny beach with an equally tiny path leading up the cliff, and I run the boat onto the pebbly sand. It's a beautiful little campsite, and the only landing spot as far as I can see. Thankfully there is phone service as well, at least on the very top of the cliff. The beach itself is strewn with sea-smooth driftwood, crumbling chunks of foam buoy, fragments of lobster trap and bits of green, fraying rope, so I pitch my tent on the grass, and after briefly contemplating whether the trouble of making a fire out of driftwood would be worth the comfort and happiness it would bring, decide against it and go to bed. I am now approximately halfway around the island.

Boy Afloat

Boy Afloat

Boy Afloat

ADVENTURE

Paddle power

JIM DAY/THE GUARDIAN
Sixteen-year-old Jo Simmons paddles his sea kayak in the Bonshaw River near his home. Simmons recently paddled around P.E.I. in under two weeks, camping each night close to the shoreline.

Bonshaw teenager kayaks around P.E.I. in just 12 days

Sixteen-year-old Jo Simmons of Bonshaw wanted to tackle a good challenge all on his own.

Paddling around Prince Edward Island in his sea kayak seemed a lofty enough goal to quench his thirst for a sizable personal adventure.

Days after completing the roughly 550-km circumnavigation of Canada's smallest province in just 11 days of paddling with one rest day, Simmons speaks with modest pride about his impressive feat.

"I'm just really happy to be back," he says. "It's nice to be able to say you've kayaked around a province."

Simmons, who bought his first kayak at age 12 from money he made selling worms, needed to roll up his sleeves to earn the opportunity for his recent trip that concluded on Friday.

First, he put in the time and effort to train, plopping his sea kayak into the Bonshaw River for regular two- to four-hour outings. He also did work around the home, including painting and a host of odd jobs, to earn money from his parents to get equipped for the trip. Among other purchases, Simmons bought a good life jacket, an extra paddle and a waterproof phone that floats. He also packed a diary and a waterproof bible. He needed, too, to work on his father, who was at first hesitant to give the teenager the green light to embark on the considerable solo kayak trek.

Simmons says he eventually convinced his father, Jonathan, that he had the commitment, responsibility and ability to take on the paddling journey.

"I don't think he had to convince me," Jessica noted of her son, Jo.

"When he had the idea, I thought he's coming up to being a man and he needs that challenge."

Still, both mom and dad followed their boy's progress closely with a healthy bit of anxiety.

Jo would check in with his parents each night after pulling his kayak out of the water, and again in the morning before setting off for his daily 10 to 12 hours of paddling.

He fueled the start of each daily paddle with a "really, really gross" protein shake for breakfast.

He ate lunch, consisting of dried fruit, meat and chocolate bars (he polished off more than 50 Snickers), while paddling.

On land, before hitting the tent early for sleep that would always come easy, Jo ate instant meals for supper, adding boiling water to rice, macaroni and cheese meals and powdered soups.

The trip would trim 10 pounds from Jo, dropping the gangly teen to 110 pounds, and leaving him "eating constantly" since returning home.

The excursion wasn't without a mishap or two. Just five days in, one foot brace broke on the kayak.

A couple of days later, the vessel capsized. Jo couldn't get back in, so he needed to swim the boat back to shore.

Fortunately, the paddler didn't lose any essential supplies.

Wind was a 50/50 proposition: half the time at his back, the other half in his face.

He had a few blisters on his hands, but muscle soreness was minimal, certainly far less than he had anticipated.

At the halfway point of his trip at Cavendish Beach, his parents drove out to restock the food supply.

At the end point, mom and dad had plenty of praise to offer up to their son.

"I never thought he wouldn't do it," says Jessica.

"I'm happy that he is home and I am proud of him."

The second oldest of five, Jo has also filled his siblings with admiration.

"It's pretty amazing," nine-year-old Toby says of his brother's triumphant paddle.

Adds sister Maya, who is 12: "I'm proud of him."

Jo has no burning desire to get back in his kayak for now.

However, he is contemplating his next adventure.

"It definitely gets your mind thinking," he says.

Boy Afloat

Day Seven

Sunday August 14th 2016
New London Bay to Oulton's Island (approximately 57km)
South-Westerly Wind 25km/h (gusting to 42km/h)

I wake up several times during the night to the sound of rain beating against the tent. Ordinarily, the gentle drumming of precipitation is a lovely, comforting, and relaxing sound and indeed, if I had been on one of those obligation-free camping trips, I would simply have smiled at the sound, wriggled deeper into the folds of my warm sleeping bag and fallen asleep for another couple of hours. However, when you know that you will soon be forced to rise, take down your soaking wet tent in the darkness and rain, put on a cold, clammy lifejacket and try to stomach the bottle of stale water mixed with lumpy, brown sludge that is your breakfast before paddling off into the mist, the sound is not so pleasant. I can only put it off for so long though, and eventually my excuse of 'it might clear up in the next half hour' ceases to deceive me. After a brief and unsuccessful attempt at fixing my foot-brace by means of a drift-wood contraption, I set off into the misting rain.

    Once I'm on the water, it's actually quite nice. The sun never manages to penetrate the clouds, so everything is dark and shadowy; a low-lying mist hangs over the water and makes the houses on the shore look ghostly. The rain, which helps to keep me cool, alternates between a gentle, fuzzy, hair-dusting drizzle, and a heavy, drumming downpour. It's vastly different from any conditions I have encountered so far, and I love it. I sing hymns, very badly and out of tune I am sure. Perhaps someone thought they heard a ghost crying out across the water that day and upon squinting out to sea, saw a figure gliding across the waves. Perhaps they still get goose-bumps when they think of it.

    I eventually reach the spot at which I have to leave the mainland and head out toward the first of a long string of islands that lie along the mouth of Malpeque Bay. I can barely see the first island (Hog Island) through the mist; it appears and disappears as the fog is shifted and blown. Before I cross, I try to get my compass out, just in case. I have to lean back and contort my arm into a painful position in order to grope around inside the day hatch, but after a few painful minutes of finding nothing but flashlights, dried fruit and Snickers bars, I slap the day hatch cover closed and continue on without the compass. I eat a Snickers bar though.

As I head toward Hog Island, the wind and waves begin to pick up considerably. Because of the fog, when I reach the island I try to stay close to the shore, but this means that I'm in fairly shallow water and the waves are bigger than I would like. The weather conditions get less and less fun and more and more scary as I continue. By the time I reach island number two, I've *almost* tipped many times. I open a packet of crackers in a short lull, and instantly see a huge wave roaring toward me. Unwittingly I've stopped right on top of a very shallow sandbar, and when waves hit such a bar they double in size very quickly. I drop the crackers into my lap and quickly grab my paddle but it's too late. The wave hits the kayak side-on and I only have time to let a surprised expression flicker across my face before I am deposited into the sea.

I don't even think to try to roll. If I had kept my head, I probably could have pushed against the shallow bottom with my paddle and so gotten up again, but I don't; I just get out as quickly as possible and grab the few things that are floating away. Thankfully, almost everything is attached to the deck securely, but unfortunately, the crackers have completely disappeared and would almost definitely be inedible. Although I'm quite far away from the shore, I am able to stand up, and the water only reaches my chest. I am unable, however, to get back into the boat. When I try to pump the water out, another huge wave comes, lifting me off my feet and filling the kayak even more. I decide to wade for the shore, but after a couple of steps, the water becomes very deep and I have to swim, pulling the boat behind me; thankfully the waves help me along, and thankfully I didn't tip when I was farther away from land.

It isn't that cold while I'm in the water, but as soon as I step, completely soaked, onto the beach, the frigid wind hits me and boy, is it cold! I pull my wet and very heavy sweater and shirt off and pull on a dry top but I'm no warmer. I'm beginning to shiver uncontrollably and, not sure what else to do, I get my sleeping bag out and crawl inside. Although the sleeping bag is far from waterproof and begins to get more and more waterlogged as the pouring rain soaks into it (picture an engorged slug), I slowly begin to warm up. I call Dad in order to alert him of my predicament (thankfully there is service out there), and he tells me to put the tent up and get warm inside that. He says that he will drive around to the shore opposite the island and bring me some dry clothes, as basically everything I have is soaked.

I discovered later that I called Dad just as he was leaving church, and in his desire to reach me quickly, he forgot that his guitar case was sitting in front of the van and so drove over it...

What follows is a mad rush of damp, sandy coldness. I put up the tent very badly behind a dune, empty the kayak of water so that I can pull it away from the waves, and then sit inside my tent eating fistfuls of Snickers bars and changing into semi-dry clothes. Then I take the tent back down and stuff it and my soaked, sandy, bulging sleeping bag into the kayak, put all my wet clothes back on top of my dry-ish ones for extra warmth and drag the waterlogged kayak across the island.

At one point, after dragging the boat about a quarter of the way across, I go back for something and after getting it, can't find my kayak again among the dunes and sand grass. I spend a harrowing five minutes looking everywhere for my bright red and yellow boat before the obvious idea of simply following the deep furrow the kayak-keel made as it was dragged across the sand occurs to me. Passing through the early stages of hypothermia really does take the intellectual stability out of you.

I eventually reach the far side of the island, and begin to paddle through the mist in the direction of a little fishing harbor. I'm not sure exactly where it is until I see our van drive out onto the pier with shining headlights. Dad is waiting for me with a warm van, a huge pile of assorted dry clothing, a piping-hot bowl of tomato soup and a generous, quivering wedge of raspberry-Jell-O pie. I sit in the van stuffing my thawing face while Dad cleans and de-sands my tent, tries to dry some of my clothing and generally cleans up my boat. I use the car to charge my phone and also try to charge my waterproof camera only to discover that a combination of cold temperatures, salty water and sand has killed it.

    I continue on, but this time on the shoreward side of the islands. This decision, while safer, is not without its drawbacks. It is shallow and hard to navigate in the mist, and I constantly have to get out of the boat and drag it across acre-long mudflats and bars. There are long lines of baskets here and there, suspended by buoys near the surface of the water. Shellfish? Shrimp? Some kind of salt water plant? As it begins to get dark, I can see the beautiful lights of Alberton shining across the deepening water. I head for them, and finally land on the shore of Oulton Island which is just opposite Alberton.

    After making my little camping spot as nice as possible (this involves dragging a lot of logs, snapping a lot of branches, removing a lot of stones and making a rather wobbly ramp out of driftwood), I decide to paddle over to Alberton. It's pitch-black and the water is fairly choppy, but the twinkling lights look so lovely and inviting across the water that I just have to. Alberton is completely deserted; I don't see so much as a single human being. I wander around for a few minutes, munching a Snickers bar, then paddle back out of the harbor beneath the huge shadows of the gently rocking fishing boats and (after briefly losing my campsite) tie my boat to a tree, make myself some macaroni and cheese, get into my tent and zip the tent flap closed against the night.

    It's amazing how safe you feel inside a tent. Although the walls are made of thin cloth and the whole structure could be torn apart in a matter of seconds by a falling branch or a smallish animal with a craving for chocolate bars, you feel invincible inside a tent with the flashlight on. The light shines out from within the warm, bright, safe interior casting a faint, orangey glow on the creaking trees.

Boy Afloat

Day Eight

Monday August 15th 2016
Oulton's Island to Waterford (approximately 35km)
North-Easterly Wind 15km/h

The coastline is pretty long and boring on the way up to North Cape, and the wind is against me the whole way. The fact that I can see the North Cape windmills when I am still hours away gives me false hope and makes the paddle even more depressing.

    I had been warned by Mr. Hicks that the current around North Cape can be somewhat dangerous, but when I do finally get there, the only problem is that the water is very shallow and it is a job not to get stuck. There are a lot of people on the beach making the most of the scenic photo I create, and so I carefully maneuver around the bars, careful not to make a fool of myself.

    There is an interpretive center at North Cape, complete with its own gift shop and restaurant, and so while the lady in the gift shop kindly re-charges my phone, I decide to have lunch at the *Wind and Reef Seafood Restaurant*. I must look a sight coming into the fairly fancy restaurant with damp splash pants, sandy water-shoes and of course the ever-present salt-encrusted hair, and indeed the lady who serves me is rather terse and condescending. I pick the cheapest thing on the menu which turns out to be a delicious Kaiser roll burger, and take my time in order to savor the experience. After collecting every last smidgen of detectable and delectable coleslaw with my fingers, I pay at the counter, grab a couple of exit-mints, recover my recharged phone and head back for the boat.

    Since the wind is behind my back now that I have passed North Cape and changed directions entirely, I try to make the most of it and paddle as fast as possible. The water is as still and clear as glass, so I am able to really skim along. As the sun begins to set, lots of motor boats head toward their harbors, and I almost get run over at one point by a large boat that is crammed with people. I have to back-paddle rather fast in order to escape it. A lady shouts, "Look, a kayaker!" just as the surge of back-wash threatens to capsize me.

The sun begins to set in a lovely sky-streaking, sea-staining wash, bathing me and my kayak in a warm, orangey glow and making the famous red cliffs even redder. Unfortunately, I am too worried to fully appreciate the beauty, as there do not appear to be any breaks in the cliff I am paddling beneath. The sun gets lower and lower and I have to strain my eyes in order to scan the shore for a suitable tent-spot. Eventually, after about thirty minutes of anxious shore-scanning, I spot a tiny sliver of pebbly beach squashed between the cliffs and come to rest with a crunch on the shore. I have to carry my tent and gear up a steep, crumbly slope in order to reach the grassy top, but there is a nice view and a gentle sea-breeze up there, and it doesn't take me long to drift off to sleep.

During the night, I wake to the sound of waves slapping against the cliff, and I hurriedly crumble down the cliff in my pajamas to make sure the boat is still on the beach. It is, but just in case, I pull it even higher.

Day Nine

Tuesday August 16th 2016
Waterford to Cedar Dunes Provincial Park (approximately 60km)
South-Westerly Wind 10-15km/h

The next day is the hottest by far, and I slather myself with sunscreen and try to drink lots of water - the fact that it's warm and salty doesn't help. I'm running out of snack-foods now, and so I try not to eat so many Snickers bars, but it's hard, very hard.

The whole coastline is so uniform that I quickly lose track of where I am. I stop briefly on a small beach to stretch my legs and have a quick bite. I check my phone for a signal. Everything is fine, so I set off once more only to realize after a few minutes that my phone is no longer in the pocket of my lifejacket. I quickly rush back to the beach and scan the sand and surf. No phone. Worried, I start to run around checking every spot on the shore. No phone. My panic slowly mounts and it is incredibly difficult for me to remind myself that I must remain calm. Let me give you an idea of the sorts of things that run through my head.

The phone is gone - no, no. No! Remain calm; you'll never succeed if you're all panicky. That's what they say in the survival manuals. OK, ok, deeeep breaths... Oh no, no, no! It's not on the beach, not in the surf, not out at sea! What am I going to do?! Think, think... I could keep going and phone Dad from the campsite up ahead, but then I won't be able to continue unless he brings me another phone. It was an expensive piece of kit! What did you lose it for? Don't panic, think, think, think... Well, I suppose I could give Dad a ring and ask him what I should... You utter idiot, don't be a fool. Well it was kind of funny. Aghh! Think, don't crack jokes! I could wait here until Dad calls me and then I might hear the ring. Yes, but if you don't hear it then he will be super worried and call the Coast Guard! Oh no! Whose idea was it to bring a phone anyway? It has brought me nothing but troub- All right... Calm, calm... It's not on the beach, so it must be out at sea somewhere. Somewhere... Oh, what an idiot I was not to zip my pocket closed! Don't worry about that now - think!'

Eventually, I realize that the phone must have fallen into the sea, and so I take to the water and sit tight for a minute or two hoping that the boat will follow the same path the phone did. The boat drifts toward some rocks just off the shore and my phone is floating right beside them. As Mr. Hicks would have pointed out had he been there, I'm smarter than I look.

I paddle on happily, closer to the coast, which makes the paddle more interesting. The coast is composed of cool rock formations - smooth, knobbly, hollowed-out sandstone that is fascinating to look at. I pass a family hiking up to their waists in water and ask them if they know how far it is to West Point Campground, where I intend to spend the night. They have no idea. I continue on, always thinking that the campground must be just around the next bend, until finally, I see a black and white striped lighthouse and… there it is.

It is really nice to once more be amongst people, and I pull my boat onto the sand and wander toward the gate in a contented state of mind. Dad has already paid for my plot over the phone, but when I let them know that I'm the person who is collecting the campsite, they look at me strangely and hesitantly hand over the necessary paperwork.

Tying some paracord to the front bungee of my kayak, I drag it across the campsite to my little spot, where I then set up everything in as homey a way as possible. Apparently, there's a storm coming, and I may need to spend two nights here while weathering it out. I don't particularly mind. I could use the break. I cook up an Uncle Ben's rice packet and then wander around checking things out. 'Beware of Poison Ivy' signs are everywhere, and I also see more wild rabbits than I have anywhere else on PEI. I have a shower before bed and am rather disappointed with the result. It is one of those showers which releases a barely detectable dribble when you press the stiff, rusty, timed button, and that has a distinct temperature pattern that is followed faithfully every single time. Cold. Warm. Tepid. Cold.

Day Ten

Wednesday August 17th 2016
Cedar Dunes Provincial Park to Cedar Dunes Provincial Park
(approximately 0km)
30km/hr. winds gusting to 54km/hr.

For the first time in what seems like an age, I am able to sleep in. All the early risings of the past nine days seem to catch up to me and to be honest, the day is a fifty-fifty split between sleep and a sort of dull, heavy lidded, partially-mobile state. The rain also alternates between a heavy downpour and a light drizzle. When awake, I lie in my tent, reading my Waterproof Bible and slowly nibbling away at my fast diminishing supply of Snickers bars.

    I do explore a little bit as well and discover a lovely little restaurant called *The Catch*. Although the burger I have is delicious, it is a rather lonely meal, and I miss having someone to argue with over the quality of the fries and coleslaw. As Mr. Hicks says, eating is supposed to be a social activity. I discover another building on the campsite I hadn't seen before that contains both washing and drying machines as well as *real* showers. I make use of both and so am able to wash and dry all the clothes that I stupidly left out on my paracord clothesline to dry the night before.

Boy Afloat

Day Eleven

Thursday August 18th 2016
Cedar Dunes Provincial park to Union Corner (approximately 58km)
South-Westerly Wind 15km/hr.

Although it's still windy, foggy and drizzly, I decide to continue. Dad has asked me to stay close to the shore as I paddle around Egmont Bay, but this proves difficult as the large waves then crash heavily into the side of my boat. After almost flipping once or twice, I decide to cut across the top of Egmont Bay, thereby heading into the wind and waves and into the deeper water which is safer; I don't want to relive my experience of capsizing. Although the crossing is scary and hairy, the wind slowly dies down as I reach the far shore, and by the time I'm paddling south, down the eastern side of the bay, the paddling conditions are perfect. I pass lots of fishing boats, each surrounded with their own little cloud of raucous seagulls, and I pass harbors, lots of them. Somehow though, there are more harbors on the coast than there are on the map, and so I quickly become confused. I actually get tricked into thinking that I am hours away from the Cape Egmont Lighthouse, and at one point even believe that the distant coast of New Brunswick is where I should be headed. When the much-desired lighthouse suddenly pops into view, I am greatly relieved and encouraged.

As I continue on toward Summerside, I hear the sound of bagpipes, and then notice a crowd of people all dancing to bagpipe music in a field. Why they are dancing I can't quite make out; perhaps it's a wedding or something. As I approach Union Corner a vast mass of dark cloud and fog suddenly blocks out the sun and everything instantly gets deathly dark and still. I pull a jacket on over my T-shirt, and as soon as I finish zipping it up, the rain just buckets down. It is so thick and dark that I can't even see the shore which is only a couple hundred feet away. After about two minutes of solid rain the clouds pass on, the rain trickles out, the sun shines down again and I am able to take my jacket back off. I can't help wondering what happened to the bagpiping party.

I pass people chest deep in water, towing plastic totes behind them via tethers of string and picking things out of the sand. I wonder what they're doing, but whatever it is, they look rather guilty as I paddle past and don't offer so much as a nod. I stop at a little beach just short of Summerside, although it's still fairly early. I want to cut across Bedeque Bay but don't have enough time tonight. I pitch my tent on a lovely grassy promontory of rock overlooking the bay. It's a beautiful evening and I can see the Confederation Bridge on the horizon which further encourages me.

I prepare myself some salami sticks, onion gravy and instant mashed potatoes for supper, using a lot of my supplies in the belief that I'll be home soon. I don't add enough liquid to the onion soup though, and the meal is far too salty for me to comfortably consume. I eat most of it anyway and then wash my dishes in the sea using sand as a scrubbing brush.

Before I close the tent flap against the mosquitos (this is the first campsite that has had that issue), I open my day hatch and scrabble around for a Snickers. There are NO MORE left. I stand beside the boat in shock and swallow several times before tearing my eyes away from the horrific sight.

It takes me a long time to get to sleep that night.

Day Twelve

Friday August 19th 2016
Union Corner to Canoe Cove (approximately 60km)

I set out dark and early on the Bedeque Bay crossing. To be completely honest, it is a very dodgy, dangerous and frightening crossing as the waves are at my back and very big. Because of this, I make the crossing in no time, but have to stop briefly at a little rocky cove beneath the Seacowhead Lighthouse to regain my nerve before heading over to the Confederation Bridge.

The Confederation Bridge. Wow, is it amazing. As I pass directly under the huge, concrete structure, the air suddenly grows chill and the wind whistles menacingly about my ears. The waves slosh and slap together, creating a mish-mash of wave action that makes it difficult to hold my position long enough to get a good look at the imposing concrete spans. After passing beneath the bridge, the waves suddenly rocket me from behind, shooting me forward at an absolutely incredible pace. That sudden, unexpected rush of water produces a speed that is definitely the fastest I've ever gone in a kayak.

I stop at a little tourist information center that is making the most of its prominent position beside the bridge and the fact that it is indeed the last place on PEI in which you can buy one of those wobble-whiskered fridge-magnet lobsters. I charge my phone for the last time.

I had not thought to arrive home until Saturday but I start to entertain the idea that I might, in fact probably will, get back that very day. The wind is behind me, and I have made excellent progress. With that in mind, I spend the remainder of my money on as much food as I can, as I have run out of all my snack foods and am very hungry. I buy a triple scoop ice-cream cone, two bags of chips and a handful of assorted candy and eat all of it. A bus disgorges a crowd of Chinese tourists just as I shake the final Dorito crumbs from the corners of the bag. They proceed to take photos of every conceivable object in sight.

As I continue, I begin to get really excited. I am starting to see places that are not just another house, another stretch of red cliff or another bay, but real places I know, with familiar people I love living in them. My desire to see the next recognizable place seems to give extra power to each of my strokes, and I speed on, desperate to round the next headland and spot the next old friend. I phone Dad to let him know that I will be arriving at Canoe Cove in about two hours and then paddle impatiently onward. I pass the beautiful village of Victoria-by-the-Sea, where I often go with my family in the heat of summer in order to jump off the dock. It's also the town in which I worked through the summer, siding and insulating and decking in order to buy my kayak and gear.

I pass Argyle Shore, a lovely little beach only five minutes away from our house. When my family comes here to swim we always turn right and walk down the beach until we come to a little, secret, rock enclosed, white-sand beach, perfect for swimming.

I flail madly onward. I feel like I'm going sooo slowly and the coast is just crawling by. Every once in a while, I throw down my paddle, grab my hair and shout "Aaarrgghh!" This doesn't help me much. I have to phone Dad again in order to tell him that I'll be a little later than I anticipated, and then continue. When I pass a headland and see the spot where I'm sure Canoe Cove is located, far away on the distant horizon, I lay my head down on my spray deck and almost cry.

Just before I phone Dad again to tell him I'll be even later, however, I look toward the shore. Then I look again. And again. There are several gazebo-ish things on top of the cliff. There is also a long building there and a lot of people on the nearby beach. Canoe Cove. Right beside me and I almost passed it entirely and started the whole trip again! I point the nose of my boat for the shore and paddle like never before. This only lasts about thirty seconds though, for the wind is dead against me, and I soon get tired. I keep scanning the beach for signs of my family but there are none. When I finally get close, I see them just running onto the sand. I wave my bright yellow paddle in the air.

Boy Afloat

Picture nine people running across a crowded and very sunny beach late in the afternoon. They are all trying to sprint straight through the many tide-pools that crisscross the beach, soaking themselves and sending up sheets of salt water that glint and shine against the sun. My little brother Toby appears to be yelling and punching his fist into the air as he hurtles into the water.

The oldest fellow is a short, stout man with almost no hair on his perfectly smooth, shiny head. He is the sort of person who doesn't normally run full-tilt through tide-pools, and he almost stops when he reaches the middle section, as the water is beginning to lap around his waist. This is Mr. Peter Hicks, and I think he is having second thoughts about things.

I leap out of my boat and charge through the shallow surf towards my family. Nathan is the first to reach me, and we give each other a big hug. He has a giant grin across his face, like me I suppose, and he doesn't look in the least disappointed that I haven't managed to kill myself; in fact, he looks glad that I haven't. Maya and Toby are close behind him, yelling and shouting and jumping around like little fleas, clinging onto me like fleas as well.

Miwa, who is leaving for Japan tomorrow, runs up behind them looking serious but excited, camera at the ready. She has been in Prince Edward Island for the two weeks I have been kayaking around it, and so will have an interesting perspective of Canada to bring back to her homeland: *"Yes, it is all as true as they say, all the stories about primitive, shirtless natives spending their time kayaking around the North American coastline, risking life and limb in the never-ending struggle for daily survival, foregoing the comforts of civilization in order to appease their innate yearnings for the fierce, undomesticated wilderness... I even have the photos to prove it."*

And then the adults come. Mrs. Hicks gives me a big hug even though my life jacket is soaking wet and tells me how happy and proud she is to see me; Mr. Hicks, drenched from the waist down but smiling and chuckling broadly in his own cheerful way, makes several good-hearted comments about how thin I've gotten, how my face looks like a bowl of raspberry custard and how he almost drowned on his journey across the tide pool; Mum, hugging me so hard that I am glad for the extra lifejacket padding; and Dad, peaceful and relaxed for what must be the first time in weeks, telling other beachgoers how 'He weighed several hundred pounds before he left you know.'

    I don't really remember what else we said as we all drifted back toward the car park. I just remember that everyone was grinning from ear to ear and laughing and taking pictures and asking questions and answering mine, and that then everyone was carrying my gear and boat towards the van, so that I didn't have to do anything anymore.

    I was supremely happy. Happy that the trip was over, yes, but also happy that I had parents who loved me, siblings who appreciated me, friends who cared about me, a God who had protected me and would continue to do so - and I realized then, as I didn't at the beginning of my trip, just how blessed I was. When I started, I was eager to leave, to get away from my home and to explore. Now I just wanted to leave exploring, go home, and sleep for several days.

I also wanted something decent to eat.

A juicy peach, for example...

Or a Snickers bar.

Epilogue

"Hey, Dad?"

"Yep."

"Thanks for letting me do the trip."

"You are very welcome. Oh! wait a second Jo. I was, um, well, I was wondering about something."

"Yes?"

"Do you have any, you know, any other trips, adventures, excursions, journeys, anything at all in mind?"

"No, not really. I would just kind of like to relax and take it easy for a bit."

"Come on, you've got to have something in the works."

"No, not really."

"Nothing? Nothing at all?"

"Nope."

"Hmm… Well I guess I'll let you think it over for a bit, you don't need to come up with anything right away."

"That's good to hear."

Boy Afloat

Supplies list

-Kayak

Kayak

2 Paddles

Neoprene spray skirt

PFD (Personal Floatation Device)

-Thingies

Maps

Bilge pump

Compass

Sun screen

Knife/Multi tool

Camera with batteries and charger

Tripod (suction)

Waterproof flashlight

Headlamp

Extra batteries

Lip balm

Pain reliever

Towel

Hand sanitizer

Dry bags

Carabineer clips (to attach things to the deck)

Shelter

Tent

Ground sheet

Sleeping bag

Food and water

Stove with fuel

Lighters

Water bottles

Cookware

Spork

Cleaning supplies

Breakfast

Chocolate flavoured protein powder

Lunch

Snickers bars

Dried fruit

Granola bars

Pepperoni sticks

Packs of crackers

Powerade

Supper

Boxes of Kraft dinner

Box of onion soup

Box of chicken noodle soup

Packets of instant rice

Packets of instant mashed potatoes

Container of mixed spices

Bottle of olive oil

Parmesan cheese

Clothing

Kayaking gloves

Sun hat

Sun glasses

Water shoes

Sandals

Rain jacket

Rain pants

Swim trunks

Normal clothing

Safety

First-Aid kit

Waterproof phone and charger

Whistle

Waterproof GPS with extra batteries

NNNN (Not Necessary Nevertheless Nice)

Waterproof Bible

Notebook with pens

Waterproof camera

Boy Afloat

Printed in Great Britain
by Amazon